American Pages

The publication of this book is made possible by a grant from the Bulgarian Writers' Union.

Dora Bonewa

BOZHIDAR BOZHILOV

American Pages

Translated by

Cornelia Bozhilova

OHIO UNIVERSITY PRESS

Chicago   Athens, Ohio   London

International Poetry Series
Volume V

Second Printing, Ohio University Press 1980

Library of Congress Card Catalog Number 80-83427
ISBN 0-8214-0596-9 clothbound
ISBN 0-8214-0597-7 paperbound

Foreword

This is the fifth book in the International Poetry
Forum's Byblos Series. The first was Marco
Antonio Montes de Oca's THE HEART OF THE
FLUTE translated by Laura Villaseñor with an
introduction by Octavio Paz. The second was
Artur Lundkvist's AGADIR translated and with
an introduction by William Jay Smith and Leif
Sjöberg. Yannis Ritsos' SUBTERRANEAN
HORSES in a translation by Minas Savvas and
with an introduction by Vassilis Vassilikos was
the third selection. The fourth selection was
Lyubomir Levchev's THE MYSTERIOUS MAN
translated by Vladimir Phillipov. The present
volume is in the same tradition of providing the
best translations of some of the most significant
poets in the world for an audience that would
not otherwise be able to read them in their own
languages.

Samuel Hazo
Director

Contents

Ode to Noise

And what strength have we
to fight noise?

The sea roars all the time,
even when the wind dribbles.
In the forest, branches and leaves rustle.
Bees hum in dark swarms like stars.

But in hospitals and cemeteries
it's quiet.

My heart beats.
Outside my house
trams, buses, people rumble.

My noisy little girls
really enjoy talking, crying, laughing.
My wife says the same old things
and sings a hymn with the vacuum cleaner.

A hunk of bread hears the noise
my old mother makes
with a knife and fork and butter frying.
On my typewriter I tap an ode
to the sweet, incessant noise
of rhythm and rhymes which otherwise
would melt silently
into nothing.

Ars Poetica

"Being a poet isn't enough—
you must be in love"
BOALO

Boalo, you taught me a lot.
Now I understand.
But all those years ago I couldn't see
why they called somebody a poet,
much less
why, perhaps,
they called me a poet.

But I've always been in love
with ideas
and being young.
I've loved the leaves on trees,
April nights,
young girls,
duty.
And for so many years
I've been in love with you,
my obsession,
my contentment.

Not knowing
how to write poems,
I live them.

Full Circle

for Cornelia

Spring will come. Spring will go.
I was young. Now no more. I'll grow old.
And I'll die. And there will be nothing left
of you and me, nothing left
except those poems in which
spring will come and go.
I shall be young, then I'll grow old,
and die, and there will be nothing left
of you and me, nothing
but love.

Men of the World

I look at them with fear
and maybe with respect.
There is dust in their hair.
Their eyes shift.
They look for hardship.
And cross a continent on foot.
The fortuity of the moment
leads them on and on.
They are hungry.
They carry packs on their backs.
When they sleep on benches, they hear
the wind blowing the trumpets of travel.
I look at them fearfully.
Can they be people?
I couldn't be like them,
I would die of weariness.

They speak of the whole world
as if it were theirs.
But they stop nowhere
and with true feeling say:
"This is my house,
my city."

They never turn back.
They don't know what it is
to love a tree,
to stand quietly looking
at its green triumph,
to have acquaintances and friends,
renewing hours . . .

They only have stations,
roads and shores.

The Dead Do Not Pass Us By

The dead do not forsake and pass us by
when we've seen them to the grave, and we depart.
It's only then the real force which lies
in their legacies cuts us to the heart.

And though their hands are resting on the flowers
passively and with a calm docility,
they gain those huge and terrifying powers
which put the lie to death's finality.

I know that you are here,
you exist, four-dimensionally.
Several people have seen you,
but vaguely
and quickly.

You exist.
Einstein explains you
simply enough.
And, of course,
rather obscurely.

He says:
From the cross section of three-dimensional figures,
a sphere
becomes a circle.
The two-dimensional circle bisected
defines a straight one-dimensional line,
and from the intersection of this line—
a geometric point.

Following the logic of these
thoughts (he adds),
the four-dimensional figure is that,
the cross-section of which
is a three-dimensional figure,
namely, a sphere.
The four-dimensional supersphere
or hypersphere,
intersected by a plane,
gives a sphere . . .

Four-dimensional world,
we see you rarely,
and then—only a few of us.

[6]

And maybe
the creatures
of the three-dimensional world
simply have no way
to understand
the four-dimensional quality of things.

Only rarely,
As an echo of a higher state,
the outlines of the superspheres,
of a superlove,
of a superpoetry,
of a superheroism,
of a superdeath
reach them.

I was young
and didn't understand
why people crash like birds
in their three-dimensional cages,
why they meet death with a song,
why they look for heart-breaking love.

In the four-dimensional world
life is not measured according to its permanence,
not according to happiness,
not according to wealth,
not according to success,
not according to defeat.
The three-dimensional logic
is powerless
before the four-dimensional thirst.

Close your eyes,
close your eyes
and feel
what once they called God,

immortality,
poetry.
Indeed it was
the fourth dimension.

There is a fourth dimension,
Everything there is simpler and more exciting.
Lips that kiss are one,
and different from those you see.

Fear

I can't remember my first love.
I've forgotten who she was.
I can't remember my best love.
I've forgotten her beauty.
I can't remember my most intense love,
or the one that hurt most.
And the most tragic love of them all,
and I have forgotten the gentlest.

Or have I forgotten? It may be a lie.

But there's one I'll never forget,
I tremble with fear of her,
I gasp and shudder,
shaking in terror
before the last.

Chicago

"Right! Don't take dollars!
Only traveler's checks!
That's Chicago, remember!
The horror of our age!"

We come to Chicago all pale.
To go out in the streets or not?
But the skyscrapers glitter,
shake stars on their shoulders.

From Lake Michigan the wind blows
as in Sliven's valley.
We look around, no blood on the ground.
And in the streets, silence.

We come to the corner. No shooting.
Some dusky women are having fun . . .
Suddenly in the darkness we go
while the wind whips the skyscrapers.

We forget all threats.
The night we finish in a noisy bar.
But timidly we advance when we get sober.
Nobody. Not a shadow of a cop.

Now, what? Opposite us, people.
They lurk behind the corner. Good Lord!
But we hear them whisper: "From jail
they've come out, didn't you get it?

They move like Chicago's bandits.
It seemed to me I saw guns under their coats."
And we were afraid of them!
Then, this the end of all our fears!

We even start to sing loud
like Chicagomen in Chicago's hour.
From Michigan a breeze lightly swings
the dark skyscrapers above us.

Night

to A. Voznesensky

To renounce—
        the example is in this.

To renounce—
        with pain, but not regretfully.
To heavens shining on without you
above the guileless oval of the sea.

But you, renouncing needs and what's unneeded,
like a nudist on deserted sands,
you will absorb part of a violetness
won by that audacity which stands
to renounce
        every moment,
                everywhere,
all dress and glory, waiting nakedly,
before a naked, carefree victory,
beneath her merciful sublimity.

There are countless women, countless suns,
there are the uncounted seas and states.
But it is only by denying them,
as a poet, that the poet penetrates them.
Fanatics stride across all complications.

But the greatness of our revolution
awaits the simple word, the clear cry.

Yet, in rejecting everything for one idea,
only then will everything reveal itself
and blend you in love and in the sea,
not as a personality, but an ideal.

Bring on the night! Change the colors,
thoughts, the bodies coupled tight!
Be an example to the suns and poets!
Bring on the simple night!

A Song of Joy

In the tunnel of the metro running towards Neuilly
a song is playing.
A tune is playing
in the metro running towards Neuilly.
A harmonica is laughing,
flinging tunes of field and wind
at the blue sky.
There's joy in the music
in the metro running toward Neuilly.

I am striding down the darkness of the tunnel
painted with multi-colored ads,
and my blood, like the light,
takes in the music
and the frightful joy
and the frightful beauty
of the melody
in the metro running towards Neuilly.

The man who made the music
suddenly is visible—
one-legged—
with harmonica.
Deprived of the sun
and its warmth,
all day he lives in the dark.
In the dark he goes on playing
the tune of joy
in the metro running towards Neuilly.

One commuter in a thousand
will tip him twenty francs.
And only when the darkness
has surrounded everything
will he leave the tunnel.

My sad friend,
don't you have tunes of sorrow?
Aren't you yourself full of sorrow?

But people have no use for it, do they?
You won't make a sou on it.
Its stocks have fallen.
In your tune there is
joy,
joy,
joy
in the darkness of the tunnel of the metro
    running
            towards Neuilly.

I forget where I am going,
yet I need to go that way,
I stop for a minute
and close my eyes.
The song grips me, the stalks of grass,
the green fingers entwine me
and toss me at the yellow sun,
to the great sky,
to the wind,
to the joyous heartbeat
of my strength, my freedom, my elation.

My friend, magician of joy,
my friend of sorrow,
along with you, I'm sad today.
I may have in me some extra sorrow,
because with my harmonica of poems
I try to shape in words
joy,
joy,
joy
in the tunnel that is solitude,
in the underground of love.

[15]

Before Leaving

I hate roaming, the farewells and the sorrow,
leaving someone behind, indifferent signals,
cold arrivals. The urge to leave again tomorrow . . .
Parting again . . .
               I hate roaming so!

With lovers of the road there is no understanding.
They shed no lovers' parting tears nor feel the sorrow.
Departure always is a loss, distance notwithstanding,
departure is a little death, though only scheduled for
      tomorrow.

Stations live
          in lovers of the road,
schedules neatly copied, pockets full of numbers,
suitcases in hand, the thresholdgod.
Old towns flash by and memory slumbers.

Lovers of the road—
            my envy grows.
Before I leave there's hell before me,
sleepless nights, flashbacks of smoke,
forebodings when roadlights flash.

The rails roll towards nowhere in my mind's eye.
The tracks tick . . .
           and I am in the dark.
The nameless stations pass my thinking by,
and once again there's someone severed from my heart.

If partings and departures are such grief
there is much that I must master . . .
Oh, lovers of the road, describe to me briefly
the way I can forget
           a little faster.

Men

Men stand alone by the river.

The water reflects the bridge and runs
down toward other men, also alone.

Who are these men
by the river, silent,
who stand all day
without the smile of a woman?

They are actors, poets, artists ...
If there is a distracting dress nearby, it will impede
the flowing of their thoughts
along the granite pier.

If she came with a kiss, it would disturb them.
If she came to talk, it would disturb them.
If she loved them, it would disturb them.
If she despised them, it would disturb them.

They are silent and alone by the river,
alone with Paris.

Poets

for Paul Engle

In a motor boat in dark water
Men undress silently.
They are no longer poets,
They are happy children.

The water circles their bodies
In a greedy embrace.
The night has never been so dangerous
Or friendly for any of them.

The black poet recalled water
With the drums of crocodiles.
He recalled the stars of hunger
In the dreams of his children.

The yellow poet recalled rain
Over the scorched black bay.
He recalled clearly the voice of death
In the organ pipes of gun barrels.

The white poet didn't recall a river.
For rivers are dry in his country.
He saw how the enemy fords
His country's free landscape.

And the poet born near this shore
Didn't recall anything because
Here he is always handsome and strong,
Thick-haired, smiling and tender.

Generation

We were the fire that consumed us.
We were only poems,
Movement,
Doubts.
Rebellious and angry,
Our time labeled us "leftists."
We had no diplomas or prizes.
We knew nothing of honors and went hungry
And had gunpowder thoughts.
We were young,
We were all young.
This is all history now.
Now the poems are in our books.
We own the ashes of the angry fire,
We recall some crazy movement.
We're sure of everything.
We won't know rebelliousness and anger again.
We're all glad to be in good health,
Glad to shelve honours and prizes at home.

Now the young are what we were.

Forgotten Poem

I once thought of a poem
And then I forgot it.
Maybe it still wasn't a poem.
I was sure it would become one.

I thought of it in the coffeehouse
As it rained outside the windows.
A good poem.
I had the feeling that I'd read it
And later forgot it.
But it's not so.

Nobody read it.
Even I couldn't read it,
It was like a child that wasn't born . . .

I strained my mind.
What was the poem that wasn't born?

What was it about?
I don't remember. I have forgotten.
But it was a good poem.

Flower

All day long I wonder what is going on at home?
What exactly is the time?
It's a bright day here, almost dusk there.
Twilight descends on the old church
While my children's joy goes rocketing over the
      cramped garden.

It's a dark night here, a clear dawn there.
I draw a breath here, I live there.
What time is it there?
Here it is evening; there it is the day.
How disturbing it is to be split!

I look at the map divided into
Time zones. A red line
Marks a mysterious border,
Marks an obscure state—
Sunday lights up here.
Monday turns blue there.

Maybe there is a coral reef
In the middle of the ocean mischievously misty,
In the middle of the ocean—dangerously distant,
Precisely dissected by this border.

Would you like us to set up a house there?
Time there would be a total illusion—
In fact, time is an eternal illusion.
On Monday I'll have a place
To write poems, and you
Will still sew on Sunday,
Just a step away from Monday.

Time would be a marvelous game there.
In fact, it is eternal.

The secret of the clover's four leaves
Would be hidden in it. Between the different days
The minutes would be identical for us,
The hours would be identical for us,
Like flowers not picked.

Relativity

A Chinese impression—
Overloaded junks come from the ocean,
Sunk to the deck in water.
They stop by the stone wharf.
Their crews come ashore.

A foreigner, musing, asks them
Whether they have sailed across the Black Sea.
The yellow sailors rebuff him.
They haven't even heard of a sea
With such a strange name
Anywhere in the world.

The foreigner then contemplates
His poems
And recalls his friends
Who are poets.

Mysterious

No one knows where his end will find him,
But I know well enough.
I'll breathe my last in a city
of fancies, imagined by me, a city
made up of streets and of houses and trees—
of skies and of torrents and constellations—
of a full dozen regular cities.

This town will merge with a street that is called Prague,
with the squares of Rome, the boulevards of Paris.
And the damp embankment slabs
will reflect the lanterns of Havana,
and Moscow's sunlight on the snow
will sprout with palms of Palermo.
The town will be reflected in the Spree
whose oil-black waters will also be present.

I see that you are smiling,
expecting mention of some lovely girl
in every corner of my imagined city,
golden-haired, or raven-haired and tanned,
or milky-white with eyes of blue or gray or brown . . .
No, you are wrong . . .
There will be just this one
who loved me, very dearly,
the one I loved,
and will be loving
but a single minute.

We'll take a Venetian gondola,
and I shall take her hand. The golden angel
will witness my oath to her—
eyes into eyes on San Marco's lovely square.

And only then I'll die . . .
And yet I won't.
For death can come about when there's a where and when.
The eyes I'll die in will have to be imagined.

Mood

Where can you be?
In which city?
Which continent?
What street?
What are you like?
Are you very small?
When will you be
here at my request?

And I shall touch
your hair
ever so lightly
and find myself in your eyes.
Then
my repose
will be untroubled
by short-term deaths.

Where can you be?
Where now?
Give me a sign!
How shall I come?
By train?
Or car?

Tell me . . .
The earth's immense,
I may be late!

Numerous towns
and streets and houses are waiting
along with verses
to fill the thickest books.

I walk from town to town
by wide shop windows.
The stars are pointing my way,
the streets lamps dance . . .
By rote I read
my life like a phantom,
but where are you?
I mustn't miss
the chance.

For it may turn to nothing.
After hearing me,
you may leave
without a word.
Find me a poem,
a portion of a poem,
my name—some letters
on a page.

VITAE

Bozhidar Bozhilov was born on April 5, 1923. He was graduated in 1946 from the Sofia University Law Faculty. The author of more than thirty books of poems, he has also written novels, plays, essays and translated English, Russian and German poetry into Bulgarian. Among his prizes are the National Literature Prize of the State of Bulgaria and the International Prize for Poetry of Italy. After having worked as a newspaper and magazine editor, he assumed his present post as the Director of the distinguished publishing house *Narodna Kultura*.

Cornelia Bozhilova is the wife of the poet and has made numerous translations of Bulgarian poetry into English.

Originally published as Volume V of the Byblos Editions, International Poetry Forum, in a limited edition of two hundred copies. The text is set in Monotype Spectrum, designed by J. van Krimpen.